Inspiring
Women
Every Day

GW00391169

November

PHILIPPIANS:
THE LETTER OF JOY
....
CATHY MADAVAN

December

THE PROMISE
OF ADVENT
....
JEN BAKER

Plus... 'Be Inspired' article, CWR Today
pages and CWR Ministry Events

Cathy Madavan

Cathy Madavan is a writer, speaker, broadcaster and coach. She often tours with Care for the Family as part of their speaking team, and is also on the board of the Kyria Network. Cathy lives on the south coast with her husband Mark, a church leader, and they have two daughters.

Jen Baker

Jen Baker is an author, speaker and pastor who has a deep love for the Bible. She has authored several books and has been involved in pastoral ministry for over 20 years, both in the US and the UK. She has also directed a charity heavily involved in assisting survivors of modern-day slavery.

Weekend

Philippians: The Letter of Joy

CATHY MADAVAN

....

Isaiah 43:1

'Do not fear, for I have redeemed you; I have summoned you by name; you are mine.' (v1)

Each morning, with a coffee within reach, I consult yesterday's to-do list. I commiserate or celebrate according to how much was achieved, and then create a new list for the day ahead. Life is busy and I will admit I even have lists of lists!

But sometimes it helps to step off the treadmill and remember what we are called to and who has called us. God has a plan for our lives! There are things only we have been distinctively designed and destined to do: there is a race that we alone can run.

As we explore themes found within the book of Philippians this month, I believe we will be inspired again by Paul's sense of calling and by the consistent friendship of the Philippian church, who Paul encouraged to be faithful in their own calling, despite the challenges they faced.

Do you ever forget that you have been called by name? What does it mean to know that Jesus has a plan and a purpose specifically for your life? Consider that calling again and pray that God will renew and re-establish His vision (and to-do list!) for your life in the days ahead.

....

Optional further reading
Deuteronomy 7:6; Matthew 4:18–22

Rejoice **always**

**Philippians
1:3–8**

'In all my prayers
for all of you, I
always pray with
joy' (v4)

I wonder what brings you joy. A roaring fire and a good book, perhaps? A live concert? Time with friends or family? It is easy to be joy-filled during the happy and comfortable times of our lives, but do we pray with joy or rejoice when things are a little trickier?

The book of Philippians is often described as the 'letter of joy', and yet Paul quickly reminded his Philippian friends that he was writing as a prisoner. His freedom had been severely curtailed, and his plans were now on hold. And yet this letter is full of unexpected joy! In fact, the words 'joy' (*chara*) and 'rejoice' (*chairo*) are used 15 times in this short letter.

So, how is this possible? It seems that Paul's joy was firstly found in *people* who he described as 'my joy and my crown' (4:1). Nothing pleased him more than seeing people grow strong in their faith. But his joy was also found in *purpose*. Paul was able to celebrate the fact that whatever happened to him, the gospel was still being shared. He encouraged his friends to 'make my joy complete' (2:2) as they fulfilled God's plans together in a way that honoured Christ.

**For prayer
and reflection**

There really is nothing like the joy of discovering God's purposes with His people. God has good plans for us! Even when our circumstances are limited, we can remain joyful because God's love and presence is always unlimited. We can know, like Paul did, that Jesus is our ultimate joy, and nothing can take that away from us. Maybe we could even write our own 'letter of joy' today, where we declare our gratitude for God's goodness, whatever our challenges might be.

**Lord, I pray with
joy today – for how
Your people and
purposes shine in
the good times but
also the tough
times. I rejoice
because You are
always good!
Amen.**

Grace Police

Philippians 1:15–19

'whether from false motives or true, Christ is preached. And because of this I rejoice.' (v18)

f there were such a thing as the Christian Thought Police, I suspect there would be no shortage of applicants to join up. It seems that whenever a celebrity speaks out about having a faith, the Thought Police are right there judging their motives and actions. Likewise, if a Christian leader falls from a position of influence or even expresses doubt about faith or a certain theological viewpoint, the Thought Police are first at the scene of the crime, ready to criticise and convict. Guilty until proven innocent.

Why would we be so quick to judge? And how would we feel if the same scrutiny was applied to us? Somehow, rather than rejoicing in people being knocked off their pedestals, let's *rejoice* when Jesus is being discussed. As Christians, let's aim instead to be known as the 'Grace Police', dispensing love, mercy and hope – building up rather than tearing down.

Paul exemplifies this stance in these verses. He admits that there are indeed people preaching with dodgy motives, and they are even stirring up trouble for him while he is in chains (v17). Yet somehow Paul trusts that God will deliver him, and he rejoices (yes, rejoices!) because at least Christ is being preached. His passion that Jesus' death and resurrection should be shared is so urgent and so wholehearted, that the rest is just tittle-tattle and distraction. His faith trumps his cynicism.

What a lesson for us. When the next person speaks about faith online or in person, let's pray that the Grace Police are the first to turn up. And let's be on the front line ourselves.

For prayer and reflection

Lord, I may not always understand or agree with others, but help me to be gracious. I rejoice because You will build Your Church and Jesus will be glorified! Amen.

Stars in the sky

Philippians 2:14–18

'I am glad and rejoice with all of you. So you too should be glad and rejoice with me.' (vv17–18)

Paul wanted to give his Philippian friends some valuable perspective, as he knew they may have been discouraged about his imprisonment. Being a young church, planted in a Roman colony, these young Christians were facing their own opposition, so Paul used his own life as an example of how to respond to hardship with joy. He explained that his incarceration had provided unexpected opportunities to share Jesus with the palace guard – those right at the centre of Caesar's empire (Phil. 1:12–13). He reminded his friends that they too could shine like stars in a dark sky, and said it was worth being poured out for Jesus in this way – in fact, he was glad, and he rejoiced with them.

This is the topsy-turvy kingdom of God. Things that the enemy would use for our harm, God will use for His and our good (Gen. 50:20). When we live in obedience to God, our mess becomes our message and our test becomes our testimony! The very places we find most difficult and stressful will quite probably be the places where we discover that we can indeed do all things through Him who gives us strength (Phil. 4:13).

In fact, it is often in our suffering that we shine in the darkness like stars, not when the sun is shining. The world is watching to see if there really is hope out there, and our lives can declare that Jesus is at work in us and through us just as much in trials as He is in the easier times. I wonder, where is He shining in the darkness for you and through you today? Where would you ask God to come and shine even more brightly in the face of disappointment or despair?

For prayer and reflection

Jesus, I rejoice that You are the light of the world that shines in the darkness. I offer You my life. Use my challenges to bring hope to others for Your glory. Amen.

CWR Ministry Events

DATE	EVENT	PLACE	PRESENTER(S)

With the extraordinary circumstances we have needed to adapt to this year, we remain committed to delivering biblically based courses and events that connect you to God, His Word and each other. Whether in person at Waverley Abbey House, or via online platforms enabling you to engage with our training from the comfort and safety of your own home, we trust you will join us and continue to be taught, inspired and encouraged by our programme of events.

For the latest information, please visit our website: **cwr.org.uk/courses** and follow us on Facebook where we will keep you up to date with dates and booking information.

We are still offering a full College programme, and value your ongoing prayers for all our staff and students at Waverley Abbey College as they continue their studies in Counselling and Spiritual Formation.

For further information and a full list of CWR's courses, seminars and events, call **(+44) 01252 784719** or visit **cwr.org.uk/courses**

You can also download our free Prayer Track, which includes weekly prayer points, from **cwr.org.uk/prayertrack**

Shifting **focus**

Philippians 4:4–7

'Rejoice in the Lord always. I will say it again: rejoice!' (v4)

S ometimes people say the strangest things. When we are facing struggles, folks might tell us to 'keep a stiff upper lip' or to 'look on the bright side'. My husband, Mark, is registered blind, and honestly, I could write a book about the inappropriate comments we've heard, including: 'Well, being blind is the easiest disability to live with, isn't it?' Seriously? What a bizarre thing to say. I wasn't aware there was an 'easy disability' scale. Even well-intentioned comments can seem dismissive and leave a bruise.

So, when Paul tells his friends to 'Rejoice in the Lord always' and then says it again, is he in danger of telling them to simply 'think happy thoughts' despite the challenges they face from their foes and the fracturing of their church relationships? On this occasion, it is quite the opposite. Alongside his wise words about their challenges, Paul is reminding or even instructing them to consciously and deliberately remember Jesus and to draw their strength from Him. It is as we pray, in every situation, that we are able to give our anxieties to Him and regain our gentleness and peace.

Paul encourages us that God's peace will guard our hearts if we focus on God more than our problems or our differences. He is bigger than on our understanding and as we fix our eyes on Him, we will be calmer, more forgiving and more resilient. It truly is a discipline to rejoice rather than to reject others. It is a decision to present our requests to God rather than to present our complaints to our friends. But it has to be worth it – to know God's peace, presence and protection for our hearts and minds.

For prayer and reflection

Lord, I choose to rejoice in You today and to give You all my anxieties and requests. Guard my heart and mind with Your peace that transcends all understanding. Amen.

Accepting the **gift**

'I rejoiced greatly in the Lord that at last you renewed your concern for me.' (v10)

The Philippian church were Paul's faithful friends and supporters, who upon hearing he was being held as a prisoner, collected money to support him and sent it with one of their members, Epaphroditus. His letter back to them clearly demonstrates his appreciation for their generosity and care. He poured himself out for them, but they, in turn, poured themselves out for him.

I am not sure how easy you find it to receive gifts, compliments or support. Over the years, due to Mark's blindness, we have had to accept help with lifts, DIY and prayer when it's hard. Similarly, as a woman in itinerant ministry, I have had to learn to accept financial support to be able to do what I do. I will be honest and say that I found this hard for a while – I enjoy giving to others, but am not quite as comfortable asking for things.

Paul's words here are wise and helpful. Although he rejoices in his friends' concern for him and is grateful for it, he has also learned to be content in every circumstance. Is he blessed by their gifts? Yes. Is his future still uncertain? Yes. Ultimately, he has to trust God for His provision. We will learn to be content when we trust that God will give us what we need, and when we accept that He delights in using His people. One Christian has enough because another Christian has been generous. It's a wonderful virtuous circle.

The challenge then is to give joyfully, but to also rejoice when people are generous with us. We can gladly share with others our time, money and prayer, but sometimes we are the ones who need to humbly and gratefully receive the blessing.

For prayer and reflection

Heavenly Father, I rejoice because I can trust You to provide for me. Help me to joyfully bless others and thank You for the many blessings I have received. Amen.

Chains

....

Galatians 5:1

'It is for freedom that Christ has set us free. Stand firm, then, and do not let yourselves be burdened again by a yoke of slavery.' (v1)

As we read about Paul being in chains for the gospel, we rightly remember those brothers and sisters around the world who are persecuted, held prisoner or even tortured for their faith today. These faithful men and women defend their faith and share their freedom in Christ, even when it costs them their own liberty – or their lives.

We are not persecuted in the same way, but we should also defend and share our faith – as we have the freedom to do so. God may have released us from more metaphorical 'chains', limitations and disappointments, but we now know what it is to be forgiven and free in Christ.

God still brings breakthrough and liberty today. He releases people into His mercy and love. We cannot free ourselves from sin. We cannot shake off the chains of our past alone. But grace sets us free, to then become messengers of this life-giving freedom for others.

Where do you still need more freedom today? Are there places where you feel limited or held back? How can you pray for or help those who are in literal or metaphorical 'chains', especially when it is for the gospel?

....

Optional further reading

John 8:36; Luke 4:18

Pursue **Christ**

Philippians 1:12–14

'most… have become confident in the Lord and dare all the more to proclaim the gospel without fear.' (v14)

t's not that I'm a control freak, but I am indeed a girl who loves a plan. I undertake more research into our family holidays than I did for my undergraduate dissertation! By the time we turn up for a week in Yorkshire, I have maps, books, lists and reviews and I know what we must see, might see and don't really need to see, with a plan B for bad weather alternatives. I think my family love me for this. I tell myself that, anyway.

So, you can imagine, I like to help God with His strategies and solutions too. I think He loves me for this. I tell myself that anyway. I can see Him sitting there, thinking, 'Oh wow, Cathy, I hadn't thought of that plan. Good job you're here.' I tell Him how things could best play out and I explain how my prayers might most helpfully be answered. What a blessing I must be.

What if, however, our strategies are sometimes flawed? What if (newsflash) God knows more than we do? I can't imagine that Paul's strategy, when planning his missionary journeys, included imprisonment. I don't think he said, 'Well, if I can just get myself chained up, then I will have a "captive" audience of military guards changing every four hours, which means I will be able to advance the gospel right into the heart of the Roman empire.' Not his plan. And what do you know, his captivity also increased the confidence of his fellow Christians who now 'dared all the more' to share the gospel without fear!

When we ask God to advance His purposes, we might not be signing up to our own plan. But we can pray that we will dare all the more, wherever God leads us.

For prayer and reflection

Lord, You are able to use all things for Your purposes. I pray that I would proclaim You without fear through every unexpected circumstance and opportunity. Amen.

Joining **in**

Philippians 2:12–13

'for it is God who works in you to will and to act in order to fulfil his good purpose.' (v13)

W e all live by faith. We have faith that the chair will support us when we sit down. We have faith that the high court judge will dispense justice fairly and appropriately for the crime committed. We might even have faith that our football team will score more goals than their opposition. Sometimes our faith is misplaced!

Paul embodied an unwavering faith that as we pursue God, God pursues us. He has already said in Philippians 1:6 that God will complete the work He has started in us, and in today's passage he reiterates that fact. God is at work in us for His purposes, and we should be in awe and trembling at the opportunity we have to join with God in His kingdom work. Our faith is not supposed to be in others or even in our own abilities. We have a living faith that trusts that as we are obedient to God (v12) we will also be co-operating with His purposes. What an awesome privilege!

What would it mean for you to know God working in you, for His purposes, where you are today? What would more of His truth, love, justice, patience and mercy look like wherever you are? Would the conversation around the dinner table sound different? Would your workplace atmosphere change? As we are obedient to God, we have faith that God will bring transformation and that He will use *us* for His purposes.

God has given you spheres of influence where He calls you to live in obedience and faith. He has not yet finished with you or the people around you! Why not list the people and places that come to mind, and pray for more of God's presence and power? His good purposes are greater than you can begin to imagine.

For prayer and reflection

Thank You, Father, for working in me and through me. I offer You these people and places and ask that You would use me again for Your glory. Amen.

Losing to **gain**

Philippians 3:7–11

'I consider everything a loss because of the surpassing worth of knowing Christ Jesus my Lord' (v8)

Remembrance Day is a poignant day, when we pause to consider the price paid by those who willingly laid down their lives for others. The gains of freedom, justice and democracy required the tragic and costly sacrifice of so many lives. In silence, we consider what we have gained by the bravery of our armed forces, but also what somebody else has lost as a result.

In today's scripture, Paul shares how he considers everything he once held dear to be a loss compared to knowing Christ who laid down everything for us. Paul said that all things are like garbage (or excrement) compared to gaining Christ and knowing Him both in His suffering but also in His glorious resurrection.

Sometimes sacrifice is worth it. Paul had left behind an influential life in order to join the very people he had previously persecuted and the cause he had so intentionally vilified. His status and his identity had been thrown on the rubbish heap in order to know freedom in Christ. It was worth losing all things in order to gain the one thing that is above all things – Jesus.

What cost would we be prepared to pay – for others, for our values but also for our faith? Would we be prepared to let certain comforts or causes go, if it meant we knew more of Jesus? Would we give up things that were part of our status or identity even, in order to be found in Him? This kind of wholehearted surrender is not supposed to be just for the brave few; it is for all disciples who follow the Messiah who has already laid down His life for them. The world needs more heroic followers who will bring His kingdom on earth as it is in heaven.

For prayer and reflection

King Jesus, thank You for laying down Your life for me, paying the ultimate price for my forgiveness and freedom. Nothing compares to knowing You. Amen.

Eyes on **the prize**

**Philippians
3:12–16**

'I press on towards
the goal to win the
prize for which
God has called me
heavenwards in
Christ Jesus.' (v14)

'm an avid goal-setter. At the start of each year I write
down what I hope to achieve in the months ahead. I
record termly priorities, and regularly put deadlines
into my diary to stay motivated and focused. Almost
always, however, if I want to say 'yes' to one goal, there
will need to be a 'no' somewhere else. If I want to get
a bit fitter, I have to actually put my trainers on and
do some exercise. If I want to see close friends more
regularly, then other coffee dates might need to wait.
If I want to write a book, all normal routines will need
to be abandoned! In order to take hold of something,
we often have to let something else go.

Paul, whose life had been transformed by meeting
the risen Christ, says that forgetting what is past, he is
focusing on what is ahead. Although he hasn't yet taken
hold of everything God has for him, he is still pressing
on towards the goal. I love these words – 'pressing
on' and 'straining towards'. These are not half-hearted
new year's resolutions or vague promises to 'do better'
and 'try harder'. These are rock-solid goals that Paul is
pursuing with laser-like focus.

My suspicion is that most of us want to press on in our
relationship with Jesus; it is forgetting what is past that
is harder. We love the new, but we also love to hang on
to the old. We want the adventure, but some things will
need to go. Saying no somewhere will enable us to say
our best yes somewhere else. Perhaps our soul needs a
de-clutter. Maybe our priorities need a shake-up. Let's
press on and strain towards the prize waiting for us.

**For prayer
and reflection**

**Spend some time
fixing your eyes on
Jesus. What
energy or focus is
needed for you to
press on towards
Him and His
purposes? What
might you also
need to let go of?**

Spiritual Formation at Waverley Abbey College

'Spiritual Formation has broadened my concept of my heavenly Father, and strengthened my faith by challenging what I believe God is doing in every part of life. God is good, and this course helps us see our spiritual lives more clearly.' – Steve (student)

At Waverley Abbey College, our successful Spiritual Formation programme will soon be entering its third year. From the beginning, we have supported students to reach their full potential, and this year will be no different.

While engaging in knowledge and conceptual frameworks drawn from theology, psychology, social sciences, historical studies, counselling, leadership studies and psychotherapy, students also benefit from time spent in prayer and devotion.

There are many options to learn within the Spiritual Formation programme, with teaching from practitioners and academics in their field of expertise. Options include university validated Higher Education options, as well as single module choices in:

- Mentoring and Coaching
- Chaplaincy
- Pastoral Care
- Spiritual Direction

These are extraordinary times, bringing about an altered pace of life with challenges for many. The need for spiritual guidance continues, and the modules that we teach equip people with the skills and tools to help others grow and develop in their Christian faith.

To find out more, please visit waverleyabbeycollege.ac.uk/ online-open-day

Good news

Philippians 4:8–9

'if anything is excellent or praiseworthy – think about such things.' (v8)

I love how social media enables us to keep in touch with the people and organisations we care about. It's fantastic to see photos of new babies, or to share fundraising achievements with friends. If I ever need advice about anything, I can stick up a post on social media and – boom! – wisdom galore comes my way. When my house had a power cut, I asked an online community group about it, and within minutes I had information and offers of help if I was uncomfortable or alone in the dark.

But that's just one side of the coin, right? Is it just me, or is it getting harder to filter out the toxicity from our world? It's like some people have one life to live, so they decide to spend it arguing about politics online! Media coverage seems to have forgotten that there is good news out there as well as bad news. It can be overwhelming at times.

Today's beautiful verses are the ideal antidote to life's noisy, negative newsfeed. Paul encourages us to choose what we set our minds on. We don't have to allow cynicism and impurity to take residence in our brains rent-free. We can, instead, invite whatever is noble, right, pure, lovely and admirable to come in and pull up a chair. Be the landlord of your thoughts!

We might have to choose more carefully who we 'follow'. It might also mean 'blocking' what is damaging, online or offline. It certainly means evicting any gossip and grumbling from our side and trying to be excellent and praiseworthy in our thoughts, words and actions. We are not perfect, but as we dwell in God's perfect presence, we will make room for more of His *good* news.

For prayer and reflection

Renew my mind, Lord. Help me to dwell on what is noble and pure. Allow my thoughts and words to reflect more of your goodness and grace today. Amen.

Confidence

....

Psalm 71:5

'For you have been my hope, Sovereign LORD, my confidence since my youth.' (v5)

At the start of Philippians 3, Paul lists why he could be confident in his own credentials. As a Pharisee and a righteous Hebrew of Hebrews, he describes his position as 'faultless'. Humanly speaking, he had it all going for him. But, spiritually speaking, it was nothing to him anymore. His confidence was now in God.

Confidence is not a bad thing. In fact, when we lack confidence or self-esteem, we are often unable to step out into God's purposes. I know many women who are extremely competent but who are often still not confident! This means we sometimes feel underqualified for roles that would suit us well. We might fear failure or worry that we are not up to the job or the juggling of life.

True confidence, though, is not about thinking more highly of ourselves than we ought to, but is about being realistic, in accordance with our faith (Rom. 12:3). So, how do you see yourself through eyes of faith today? Can you recognise your God-given value? Are you unwrapping your spiritual gifts for Him? Your confidence is found in God, but He also has confidence in you.

....

Optional further reading

1 John 5:13–21; Jeremiah 17:7

Remain **united**

**Philippians
1:9–11**

'And this is my
prayer: that your
love may abound
more and more in
knowledge and
depth of insight'
(v9)

Paul loved the Philippian church. He described them as partners in the gospel, brothers and sisters, supporters and servants. They were generous, thoughtful and committed friends – not without their challenges, but faithful nonetheless. Their love was a witness to the work of God in their lives.

This beautiful prayer reveals that being deeply rooted in love leads to knowledge and insight, discernment and fruitfulness. Love has far greater potential than mere fluffy feelings or superficial fellowship. Paul knew that people flourish and grow fruit of righteousness and purity when they are firmly planted into a community of love.

I would definitely appreciate depth of insight and the ability to discern what is best, and I certainly want to be filled with the fruit of righteousness! But honestly, I don't always let love abound more and more. And yet that is the key that unlocks God's wisdom and purpose. The thing is, loving people is not always easy... but, biblically speaking, it is a powerful weapon. People will witness the truth of the gospel because of our love (John 13:35), and there is blessing when we dwell in unity (Psa. 133:1–3).

If Jesus' summary of all the law was to love God wholeheartedly and then to love others as well as loving ourselves, then we can assume this is the root of all righteousness and fruitfulness. So, how well are you doing on the 'love' front today? How deep are your roots into God's love? How are you growing in love for others? Imagine if we were to pray for each other that our love may abound more and more. What a powerful prayer!

**For prayer
and reflection**

**Heavenly Father,
may I grow in my
understanding of
Your love, and may
I also grow in love
for others, so that
Your purposes may
be fulfilled in me
and through me.
Amen.**

One mind, **one spirit**

Philippians 2:1–4

'make my joy complete by being like-minded, having the same love, being one in spirit and of one mind.' (v2)

Have you ever asked a rhetorical question where you already know the answer? Whether you're a parent or not, you may have asked a child, 'Do you want to sit at the table all night eating that broccoli?' Or maybe, when receiving a work of art from a toddler, you've said something like, 'Who is the best artist in the whole wide world?' It's obvious what you're getting at – you don't really need a response.

As we turn today and tomorrow to some of the best-known verses in Philippians, Paul proposes a series of suggestions that he already knows the response to. Four times in a row he effectively says, '*If* this is what you believe, then *this* should be your response.' He is leading them so they understand that their beliefs should shape their actions.

These verses remind us that having received so much grace from Christ, we are in a position to be gracious to others rather than elevating ourselves. We should guard against falling into a me-first and self-centred default position, or putting our own interests at the top of every agenda. One leader suggests that when we walk into a room, it's good to try to adopt a 'there you are' attitude rather than a 'here I am' one. Let's ask more questions than we share opinions. We can delight in the promotion and success of others and encourage others to thrive. We don't have to be the best or know best about everything.

What a witness to a divided world it would be if believers modelled being of one mind and one spirit, despite our differences. It is possible – 'if we have any encouragement from being united with Christ'.

For prayer and reflection

Help me, Lord, to value and respect others as You do. Give me eyes to see the dreams, desires and interests of those around me. May I be an encouragement to someone today. Amen.

Sing it out

**Philippians
2:5–11**

'In your
relationships with
one another, have
the same mindset
as Christ Jesus' (v5)

I am so grateful for modern worship songs. For me, there is nothing like joining with others to sing beautiful truths together. It is also refreshing to play those worship songs at home or in the car to focus on God during the day. Personally, I also have a deep love for older hymns, which often include wonderfully crafted theological insights. Can anything beat belting out the last verse of 'And Can It Be?' in two melodic parts at full blast?

Today's verses are likely to be one the earliest Christian hymns or creeds on record. They are written in such a way that the Philippian church would probably have been familiar with them. They could have been used at a communion gathering or at a baptism. But whatever the purpose, this is surely one of the finest passages of writing about Jesus we have, explaining who He is, what He did, why He did it and where He is now.

Rather than guilt-tripping his friends about their pride and selfishness (which definitely needs attention), Paul draws their attention back to Jesus with this song. He reminds them of His incredible humility and obedience and how He didn't grasp at power but now is exalted to the highest place. The sacrificial servant-heartedness of Jesus is our example when we are tempted to strive, to always be right or to win the argument.

What a wonderful reminder. We will only remain united when we remain humble. We can only truly love when we have the same mindset as Christ Jesus. In today's self-centred world, when we all wrestle with it being 'all about me', these verses really are a hymn worth singing.

**For prayer
and reflection**

**Lord Jesus, I
am grateful for
worship songs that
remind me of who
You are. Thank You
for Your humility
– may Your servant
life be an example
for me today.
Amen.**

Above and **beyond**

Philippians 2:19–30

Have you ever written a reference or a commendation for somebody? Perhaps you yourself have had to ask for a reference. I have to approach people to write endorsements for my books, which I find both unsettling and humbling! However, when we know the people concerned, we can be confident that they have our best interests at heart.

'But you know that Timothy has proved himself, because as a son with his father he has served with me' (v22)

Paul writes a wonderful endorsement of his two significant friends, Timothy and Epaphroditus. The church already knows Timothy, so it is not as if they need a character reference, but Paul is using him as a living example to underline truths he has been teaching. Timothy, who Paul loved like a son, was clearly a trustworthy man who unselfishly considered the needs of others. Perhaps he would need to tackle their disunity issues and Paul is commending him to them.

Epaphroditus, as one of their leaders, is known well too. Paul informs them how high the cost has been for him, possibly to avoid any unhelpful conclusions about his premature return, but probably because he is concerned about this godly leader and his distressing brush with death. He wants the church to embrace this man who has sacrificed and served so willingly.

It is right that we honour those who go above and beyond in any sphere of life, but particularly in the Church. It is also good to commend those in church leadership who give faithfully and serve wholeheartedly, often at great personal cost. Men and women of good character who lead and love with diligence are to be treasured and encouraged. Is there somebody you could commend or thank today?

For prayer and reflection

Thank You, Lord, for the people I know who reflect Your character. Thank You for Christlike leaders who love and give so willingly. Bless them, I pray. Amen.

The same **mind**

**Philippians
4:1–3**

'I plead with
Euodia and…
Syntyche to be of
the same mind in
the Lord.' (v2)

What a way to be remembered. These two women, who have carried responsibilities in the church alongside Paul, have clearly fallen out big time. Their division, which has been hinted at throughout the letter, is now addressed specifically and directly, with a plea for assistance in helping them over their differences.

What I find fascinating here is that Paul encourages the women to be 'of the same mind in the Lord'. He doesn't instruct them to agree with one another; in fact, he doesn't go into the details of whatever the issue is at all. His focus is on their relationship and the unity of the church family. Sometimes we all have to agree to disagree, but we can do it agreeably! It is quite possible to not think the same about every issue, but to be of one mind in the Lord. Our common goal is unity in Jesus and our shared identity as children of God is the basis of our 'one-ness'.

Without a doubt, conflict is one of the most difficult things in life to deal with. When we fall out with somebody, we might wake up with a knot in our stomach. We lose our peace when we are hurting, and it takes time to recover from harsh words, misrepresentation or rejection. We all know families, businesses or churches that have split because people could not agree or forgive. While not every issue is resolvable, Christians are called, with humility and grace, to focus on the one who asks us to be as one in mind and spirit. With help from others as needed, let's make every effort to acknowledge our differences but to avoid relationship breakdown whenever possible.

**For prayer
and reflection**

Lord Jesus, help
me to forgive
others as You have
forgiven me. Give
me courage to
overcome hurt and
to ask for help
where needed.
Make me a
peacemaker,
I pray. Amen.

Courage

....

Psalm 27:1

'The LORD is my light and my salvation – whom shall I fear? The LORD is the stronghold of my life – of whom shall I be afraid?' (v1)

When was the last time you felt afraid or out of your comfort zone? I often speak on stage in front of a lot of people, which can be scary, but there have been times when I have had to be far more courageous: dealing with a scary diagnosis, getting stranded overseas in a hurricane, being lost in a forest, and many more besides.

We all have to face our fears sometimes. And Paul was certainly facing an uncertain future as he wrote to the Philippians, in prison and in danger of losing his life. A man of faith however, he hopes and expects to have 'sufficient courage' so that Christ will be exalted, whether by life or by death (Phil. 1:20).

The Bible often encourages us to 'not fear' or to be 'strong and courageous'. God knows we will face things that are overwhelming, and sometimes the future will be uncertain. We need to remember that the Lord is our strength and light, and ask Him to intervene, but let's also take a leaf out of Paul's book and pray that we will have sufficient courage and that Christ will be exalted, whatever the outcome. A brave prayer indeed…

....

Optional further reading

Joshua 1:1–7; Isaiah 54:1–8; 1 John 4:18

Resources for you and your church's wellbeing

After some of the unprecedented challenges faced all over the world this year, perhaps many of us have been reflecting on the meaning and importance of wellbeing, in our lives and in our churches. Now that we are starting to look ahead to another new year, this is a great time to consider how to invest in your walk with God, and in your own spiritual, mental and emotional wellbeing, throughout 2021. God cares deeply for us, and that includes all aspects of our lives.

We have two series that you, your small group or your whole church can engage with to help you live well, place God at the centre, experience His *shalom* peace and goodness and the impact this has on every aspect of our wellbeing.

These Three Things and **God's Plan for Your Wellbeing** are based on sound biblical teaching around how we have been designed to depend on God to meet our every need, and that He longs to meet those needs for us. Each has been developed with an abundance of additional resources available online, including sermon outlines, small group discussion starters and videos, to enable you to really get the best out of the teaching, whether through face-to-face or virtual learning.

These Three Things

Mick Brooks, CWR

God's plan for us is to live in relationship with Him, and look to Him as the primary source of our security, self-worth and significance. Because we are made in His image, only He can satisfy our deepest longings. Through 42 daily readings, explore how we can know life in all its fullness, even when things go wrong.

God's Plan for Your Wellbeing

Dave Smith, Kingsgate Church

In this brand-new series, created with both Christians and sympathetic enquirers in mind, Dave Smith follows the wellbeing narrative of the Bible, and explores how when we discover God's plan for our wellbeing, we experience fuller understanding of His care and concern for the physical, spiritual, emotional, vocation, relational and financial areas of our lives.

PROVISONAL COVER

For prices and to purchase, visit **cwr.org.uk/store**
For more information on how to register your interest and plan to engage your groups or churches in either of these series, visit **cwr.org.uk/for-your-church**

Stand **firm**

**Philippians
1:20–26**

'Yet what shall I choose? I do not know! I am torn between the two' (vv22–23)

H ave you ever played the game, 'Would you rather?' My kids loved it for a while. The premise of this highly intellectual game (not) is that you are given a random choice, and you have to decide which you would rather. For example, you might be asked, 'Would you rather fight 100 duck-sized horses or one horse-sized duck?' Deep stuff.

Some choices in life, though, are much less funny and far more significant. Paul knows he could live, or he could die, but given the choice, he would be torn. For him, 'to live is Christ and to die is gain' (v21). The thought of being with Jesus is compelling, but he decides it would be better to remain if he could encourage others in their faith. What a choice!

Every day, we face hundreds of choices. Some are mundane, like what socks to wear, but others are more profound. We choose what to do when faced with temptation. We choose where to invest our time and money. We choose whether we serve and if we share our faith. We may choose what is easier or more desirable for us, or we may choose what gives glory to God and would benefit others the most. Our life is a series of choices and we consciously or unconsciously build what we choose.

For prayer and reflection

Thank You, Father, that you choose to love me unconditionally. Today I choose to follow You. Be with me in every decision, whether it is small or significant. Amen.

What choices are you facing today, I wonder? How might you, with faith and commitment, bring more of God's wisdom and insight into the decisions and temptations you face? In our heavenly Father's presence, we discover His peace, His purpose and His power. Perhaps we could start by choosing to spend more time in prayer with Him. Would you rather do life without Him or with Him?

Citizens of the **kingdom**

**Philippians
1:27–30**

'you stand firm in
the one Spirit,
striving together as
one for the faith of
the gospel' (v27)

When Paul instructs his friends to conduct themselves in a manner worthy of the gospel, he uses a word used to describe the behaviour expected by Roman citizens. Philippians would have been very proud of their colony, which would have been reflected in their customs, dress and civic responsibilities. Paul reminds his Philippian friends that they should be even more proud to be citizens of Christ's kingdom, and their behaviour and commitment to one another should be consistent and worthy of this high calling.

Although they are facing many struggles and fears, and despite the opposition they face, Paul encourages them to stand firm. Their unity and their conduct will be a clear signal to their oppressors, whoever they are. Paul believes that God will vindicate us, and God will save us, but he knew that to withstand the enemy, we need a united front.

The pressure is on. Our culture doesn't always encourage Christianity to thrive and we need to eliminate friendly fire in order to create a united front. Our commitment as citizens of heaven and our commitment to His great commission should be more compelling to us than any other position we hold. Let's not be so afraid of losing the roles or status given to us that we stay silent or become inconsistent. Our steadfastness and certainty can be a sign to those around us that we are serious about our faith and that our trust in God is unshakeable.

As the Church stands firm for God, we know that God stands firm with us too. He won't let us down and He is always faithful. Let's conduct ourselves in the light of that truth.

**For prayer
and reflection**

**Lord, thank You
that You stand
with churches who
face opposition
today. May we
also stand firm in
our commitment
to You, whatever
challenges arise.
Amen.**

More than enough

**Philippians
3:1–6**

'For it is we who are
the circumcision,
we who serve God
by his Spirit, who
boast in Christ
Jesus' (v3)

When I became a Christian at university, I was overwhelmed by the grace of God. I was transformed as I understood that through Jesus' life, death and resurrection, I could know forgiveness, acceptance and freedom to be everything God had made me to be. I was a new creation and it felt good. Soon, however, other messages began to creep in. Why didn't I speak in tongues? Well, perhaps I was not full of the Spirit after all. Was I hoping to speak in church? Well, women might not be given permission to do that. Where had my new-found freedom gone?

It's no wonder Paul had such harsh words for the people who were causing havoc in the Early Church, destabilising other people's confidence in God's grace-gift to them. He was almost certainly speaking about the 'Judaizers', who were confusing early Christians by adding rituals and traditions such as circumcision to the gospel message in order for people to be truly acceptable to God. Suddenly, many believed that grace was not enough after all.

But Jesus is enough. He is more than our enough. In Romans 2:28–29 we are reminded that God seeks a circumcision of the heart, not the body. Our confidence is not in laws and rituals and doing enough to gain God's approval. Jesus' death cost far too much for us to add extra hoops to jump through. Paul longed for people to come back to the truth, and he is understandably protective of those impressionable young believers.

You and I can joyfully stand firm on this truth today: Jesus has already done enough. You are accepted because He has made a way for you. What amazing grace!

**For prayer
and reflection**

**Jesus, You are the
Way, the Truth and
the Life. Thank
You for all You
accomplished on
the cross for me.
Nothing else can
set me free – I
worship You alone.
Amen.**

Leading by example

I n today's verses, a tearful Paul begs his friends to stand firm again, asking them to emulate him and others who they know are following the true gospel. Clearly there are influences – perhaps the Judaizers, although possibly others also, who are worshipping their own appetites and boasting about earthly things ('and their glory is in their shame', – 3:19).

'just as you have us as a model, keep your eyes on those who live as we do.' (3:17)

Was it arrogant for Paul to suggest that he should be a role model to others? Was he getting rather big for his boots? No – Paul lived with the Philippians, and knew they had witnessed the contrast between how he lived as a follower of Jesus and how these others behaved. Similarly, Paul also told the Corinthian church to 'imitate me, just as I imitate Christ' (1 Cor. 11:1, NLT).

This instruction is helpful for us too. We need to know the way of Christ but to also show the way of Christ in our words, actions and attitudes. Those younger in the faith should be able to learn something about following Jesus from our example. The way we serve, love and forgive others, our generosity, hospitality, prayer-life, and the way we treat people, fight oppression or serve the poor – in every area, we need to learn more from those we admire, but as we follow Christ, let's pray that others might learn from us too.

Never has this call to role-model, to nurture and disciple been more needed. We need each other to stand firm in the faith. The next generation is calling out for those who will know and show the way. We all have much to learn, but we also have much to offer. The question is, who are we imitating, and who are we discipling?

For prayer and reflection

I fix my eyes on You again today, Lord. Give me eyes to see who I can learn from, and who I can encourage to grow in faith. Amen.

Begin and end **with grace**

**Philippians
1:1–2; 4:21–23**

'Greet all God's people in Christ Jesus. The brothers and sisters who are with me send greetings.' (4:21)

How would we ever stand firm in our faith if it was not for the people around us? God gives us friends, mentors, church family, leaders and extended family who cheer us on and who we can cheer on. It's not that those relationships don't come with complications (they clearly do!), but we are not designed to do life alone. God is a God of relationship who designed His people to live in relationship with Him and with each other.

The beginning and end of Paul's letter to the Philippians are almost like a mirror image. He wants every person to receive a greeting, including the leaders and overseers and especially Caesar's household. Since Philippi was a place where veterans of Roman wars were often settled as a reward for their service, there were probably soldiers or slaves linked to the imperial household who had come to faith and joined the church. Already, within 30 years of the death and resurrection of Jesus, the gospel had penetrated the heart of the Roman Empire. The gospel knows no barriers!

Isn't the Church such a kaleidoscopic mixture of people, from all kinds of backgrounds? Isn't the body of Christ the most diverse and beautiful family in the world? Nobody is out of the reach of God. Our outreach should never be limited to people who look like us. God has no favourite socio-economic group and He longs for all to know Him.

Unsurprisingly, then, Paul's letter begins and ends on the subject of grace. It is about Jesus. Paul knows we can't stand firm or stay united alone. It is as the Spirit fills us each day, by His grace, that we can love others as He loves us.

For prayer and reflection

Your family knows no boundaries, Lord. Thank You that all are welcome. Thank You that Your grace is enough for everybody, including me. Amen.

Contentment

....

Matthew 6:25–34

'But seek first his kingdom and his righteousness, and all these things will be given to you as well.' (v33)

Some of us are worldwide experts in worrying. We worry about our family. We worry about our work. We worry about what we look like. We worry about what to do next. Our perfectionist side worries we are not doing well enough and our people-pleasing side worries we will let people down. Some days, we worry about what to worry about!

Really though, we should worry more about how worry robs us of our contentment.

It doesn't have to be this way. Paul, although in prison, learned to be content in all situations through Christ who gives him strength (Phil. 4:11). Today's verses echo this sentiment, as Jesus Himself tells us not to worry about every little circumstance. Instead of worry leading our life, Jesus directs us to keep our eyes on His kingdom and to trust Him for the other stuff.

How much more peace-filled would we be if, instead of worrying and striving, we got back to seeking God above everything else? Instead of ruminating over the past or catastrophising about the future, His presence in our present is the key to our peace. Why not seek Him first today?

....

Optional further reading
Psalm 23; Hebrews 13:5–6

An acceptable **sacrifice**

**Philippians
4:18–19**

'And my God will meet all your needs according to the riches of his glory in Christ Jesus.' (v19)

When I go out with certain friends for coffee, I know they will offer to pay. On a 'spreadsheet' level, we know that their job and my ministry command very different bank balances! It's not that they doubt my generosity (indeed I insist on paying sometimes), it is that their financial well is deeper than mine, and it actually delights them to bless me, if I am able to humbly receive that blessing.

We know how thankful Paul was for his Philippian friends and their generosity. Their sacrifice was accepted gratefully – a fragrant offering indeed. Paul's ministry was enabled as a result. But ultimately, Paul knew that their wellbeing (and his) were only possible because of the glorious riches of Christ. God's well is deeper than anybody's!

Whatever our status or position, we are all dependent upon God's goodness. Knowing that His resources are unlimited and unconditionally given should give us confidence and reassurance. We don't have to worry whether He has run out of forgiveness or whether His stock of grace has run low. It hasn't and it won't. We don't have to earn our way into His affection or face problems without His assistance. We never have to pay-as-we-go for our mistakes in life, because Christ has already paid the price for us – the ultimate acceptable sacrifice.

This is why Paul was content. His letter to his friends shared how he could rejoice always, pursue Christ, remain united and stand firm because he had learned to receive God's goodness. Our heavenly Father delights in knowing us and blessing us – we simply need to be willing to receive that blessing each day.

**For prayer
and reflection**

**Thank You, Lord,
for Paul's letter
and for teaching
me more about You
and Your family.
May I live in
humility with
others and trust
You to meet all my
needs. Amen.**

Perfect Gifts for Christmas...

Advent

Unexpected Jesus

God's people had been waiting for a Messiah for as long as they could remember, but when He arrived, He wasn't quite what they had expected. Spend each day of Advent reflecting on how Jesus transformed lives in unexpected ways. Ideal for individual or small group use.

By Anna Robbins
ISBN: 978-1-78951-258-8
£6.99

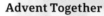

Advent Together

Journey through *Advent Together* as a family, with daily Bible readings, thoughts and activities for the everyone to enjoy. Take a look at Old Testament prophecies about Jesus, and how we can prepare to celebrate His birth.
By Steve and Bekah Legg
ISBN: 978-1-78951-265-6
£8.99

Family Devotionals

More 12-week family devotionals from the Legg family. The four titles can be read in any order.

All Together
ISBN: 978-1-78259-692-9

Time Together
ISBN: 978-1-78259-798-8

Life Together
ISBN: 978-1-78259-999-9

Growing Together
ISBN: 978-1-78951-264-9
£8.99 each

For children and young people

The Camel Who Found Christmas
The littlest camel is concerned about going to see the new king who has been born. However, on the journey he learns from Mama Camel that everyone is big enough, everyone is important enough, everyone is smart enough and everyone is special enough to meet King Jesus.
By Alexa Tewkesbury
ISBN: 978-1-78951-273-1
£1.99

50 Christmasiest Bible Stories
With colourful cartoons and his unique style of storytelling, Andy Robb brings some of the Christmasiest Bible stories to life.
By Andy Robb
ISBN: 978-1-78259-418-5
£5.99

One You, One Year
These one-year devotionals are packed with inspiring Bible readings, relevant thinking points and life changing prayers. Written in an engaging and upbeat style with specific themes, these books will encourage young people in their walk with God.

One You, One Year: 365 for Boys
ISBN: 978-1-78259-994-4

One You, One Year: 365 for Girls
ISBN: 978-1-78259-993-7
£9.99 each

Ideal for ages 10–14

For women and men

Gifts for women

Unwavering

Jen Baker explores the power of living an intentional life, and how we can make decisions boldly and confidently when we remember who we are in Christ. An encouraging and thought-provoking read for women of all ages.

By Jen Baker
ISBN: 978-1-78951-247-2
£8.99

The Beauty Within

For women of all ages, this interactive, reflective journal considers how God sees us as His daughters, and how we can cultivate an inner beauty that reflects His image.

By Rosalyn Derges
ISBN: 978-1-78259-832-9
£12.99

Gifts for men

The Code

Written by the team at Christian Vision for Men, this is a 12-point honour code for today's Christian man to live by, and respond to the call to live an uncompromised, Jesus-centred life.

By Carl Beech, Nathan Blackaby and Ian Manifold
ISBN: 978-1-78951-149-9
£8.99

Or order by post – see order form on last page

Christian living

Provisional cover

Specks and Planks

Jeff Lucas is back with another collection of touching, funny and profound stories from his years of following Jesus. These short but heart-warming anecdotes bring a disarming level of insight to everyday experiences, causing you to ponder, laugh and see life through new eyes.

By Jeff Lucas

ISBN: 978-1-78951-244-1

£8.99

God's Plan for Your Wellbeing

Drawing lessons from the life of Elijah, church leader Dave Smith looks at how we can go back to God's plan for our physical, spiritual, mental, emotional, relational, vocational and financial wellbeing. With additional free material available online, this book makes a great resource for churches and small groups to journey through together.

By Dave Smith

ISBN: 978-1-78951-279-3

£8.99

Multi-buy offers available

The Promise of Advent

JEN BAKER

A s an observer, I have witnessed the wonder of childbirth and, let's be honest, although miraculous, the experience is often messy and shrouded in the unknown. We wonder: *Who is on the other side of this agony? Will the birth go according to plan? How long will it take? Will the pain be too much?* Like bees to honey, these questions and many more swarm a new mother's mind. Mary, the mother of Jesus, would have been no different. She could not have fully understood what would be revealed on the other side of her miraculous, and presumably painful, delivery; but one thing she did realise: life would never be the same.

Birthing is a door into an unknown future. This month, many 'doors' will be opened on Advent calendars as children anticipate the surprise (usually chocolate!) on the other side. It reminds me of a people waiting for a saviour, surprised that their Messiah entered through the door of humility – as a baby who could not speak, walk, or even control His bodily functions. Today we still find this season marked by surprise packages, literally and metaphorically.

Our themed scripture (Isa. 9:6) will be our foundation as we anticipate the birth of our Saviour and the start of a new year. This child has been born 'to us': He is the ultimate gift, wrapped in the most beautiful of packaging. In Him are many promises carrying life, truth and gifts only found on the road less travelled. We will see His attributes (promises) behind the door of each day's devotion, so – as you would an Advent calendar – let's open each reflection, savour the promise and enjoy the journey.

Isaiah 9:1–7;
Revelation 3:8

'For to us a child is born' (Isa. 9:6)

For prayer and reflection

Lord, as I anticipate a busy month, I pause to meditate on Your 'packaging', arriving as a helpless baby. Help me see beyond the stress of the season to the gift of salvation. Amen.

A son is **given**

**John 3:16;
Ephesians 4:2–3**

'For God so loved the world that he gave his one and only Son'
(John 3:16)

A s a child, I thought all my dreams had come true when I received the teddy bear I wanted for Christmas. He became my best friend, though he now lives in my parents' attic bearing the scars of a child's love – with one eye and half a nose still attached to his face.

At the time, that bear was a treasure to me, but maturity changes our perspective on what counts as a prized possession. Those of us following Christ's teaching know that possessions may be meaningful but they are never eternal. Equally, one of the most profound truths from the Bible is that by giving, we also receive. This giving is occasionally sacrificial because God's gifts are not dependent on perfect conditions. In fact, giving is often found in imperfect circumstances; for example: the gift of letting a loved one go; letting a child make her own decisions; releasing our personal dream to the will of heaven; or sacrificing the gain of today for the wealth of tomorrow. This 'dark night of the soul' season may not feel like a gift but, given time, it will reveal beautiful promises only found in a season of intense testing. This paradox of promise was confirmed by God Himself when, on the cross, He demonstrated the purest of love while embracing the deepest of pain.

As we enter a season often fixed on material gifts, let's focus on a different kind of present: the gift of forgiveness, love, generosity, kindness, grace and peace – each packaged in a timeless beauty, which never fades or tarnishes. Each sacrificial gift carries a promise that the return outweighs the sacrifice... even if you are left with half a nose.

For prayer and reflection

Lord, thank You for being with me through the ups and downs of 2020. Help me be grateful for what is present, not focused on what is missing. Amen.

The **keys**

Isaiah 22:22;
Matthew
16:18–19

'what he opens no
one can shut, and
what he shuts no
one can open.'
(Isa. 22:22)

As we read on Tuesday, before baby Jesus rested on Mary's shoulder, the government was placed on His (Isa. 9:6). In the book of Matthew, we see this eternal assignment being shared with Peter, when Jesus invites him to steward the keys to the kingdom. This authority is carried out in many ways – one of the most prominent being through our words.

Prayer was never meant to be a burden or a spectator sport but instead a powerful exchange between heaven and earth – one which moves mountains, heals bodies, shatters darkness and expels the enemy. Our prayers gain access to the heights of heaven, carrying truths to the expanse of earth. By speaking the promises of God, we are unlocking a door of truth within an atmosphere of unbelief. What a privilege! But, as exciting as it sounds, there are days this responsibility may feel like a burden.

I remember as a young teenager begging my parents for a fish tank, assuring them I would be a responsible owner. They relented, and a 30-gallon tank was placed in my bedroom, complete with beautiful, exotic fish. For weeks, I enthusiastically watched the fish swim in circles, mesmerised by their beauty – and lack of memory. I fully enjoyed my newly acquired responsibility... until the tank needed cleaning; at which point, I quickly lost my enthusiasm for fish ownership.

Our attitude towards prayer can be similar; we begin enthusiastically, only to lose momentum as the 'waters get muddied' and the responsibility increases. Right now, there are doors of freedom in our communities and among our relatives that need opening. How might God be inviting you to partner with Him in bringing breakthrough?

For prayer and reflection

Praying for others is like unlocking destiny over their lives. Who needs your prayers for a new beginning? Spend a few minutes declaring promises over their life.

What's in a **name**?

Philippians 2:6–11

'at the name of Jesus every knee should bow' (v10)

Remembering names is the bane of my life on some days. It is not for lack of trying – I do – but about five years ago something shifted and I transitioned from excellent memory to 'no idea who you are' in about the same amount of time it takes a child to open their Christmas presents. To my shame, I have learned how to greet someone, have a conversation, pray with them and say goodbye without needing to say their name even once. Please tell me I am not alone in this?

I say 'to my shame' because names are extremely important. I enjoy finding meaning behind people's names and I am fascinated by the care many cultures take when naming their children. We know that the name of Jesus carries much more than five letters: it has toppled kingdoms and freed captives, comforted the grieving and calmed the storm, invited ridicule and silenced the critic. His name is above *every* other name that has ever been, or will ever be, spoken.

Throughout the following weeks, we will explore the names prophesied over a little guy born to a virgin: Wonderful Counsellor, Mighty God, Everlasting Father, Prince of Peace. Such bold names for a newborn – declared before He could speak and written before He could write. You have also had names declared over you before you took your first breath: overcomer, cherished, highly favoured, courageous and strong – to name a few. These names are not based on our feelings or circumstances but are truths etched into the pages of our story, today and throughout eternity. Any name less than these slanders our real identity as children of God, and that's something we must never forget.

For prayer and reflection

Lord, thank You for the names You have called me throughout the Bible. Help me to view myself in light of their truth today. Amen.

Choose your thoughts

For reflection: Philippians 4:4–8; 2 Corinthians 10:5

'think about such things.' (Phil. 4:8)

Even though He can do anything, God does not choose our thoughts for us. The Bible is clear that *we* are responsible for owning our thought life. Giving our thoughts free reign is like handing the house key to intruders and becoming upset when they destroy our home and steal the furniture. We need to take care not to give the enemy possession of territory that is ours to maintain. We can't always stop thoughts entering our heads, but we can choose not to entertain them.

If this is a new or challenging concept then I would encourage you to meditate on the scriptures above, especially Philippians 4:8. The word 'think' in that verse is not a one-time decision but means, in Greek, an ongoing action; or another way to say it, a lifestyle. Years ago, I had a quote in my office that said: 'Your thoughts become your words; your words become your actions; your actions become your habits; and your habits become your destiny.' Notice: our destiny begins with our thoughts. This weekend, retrieve keys you may have surrendered, take captive your thoughts and bring errant thinking in line with truth. Remember, it's *your* home.

Optional further reading

Joyce Meyer, *Battlefield of the Mind* (London: Hodder & Stoughton, 2005)

Wonderful **Counsellor**

**Jeremiah 32:17;
Colossians 2:3**

'in whom are
hidden all the
treasures of
wisdom and
knowledge.'
(Col. 2:3)

magine having free access, at any moment, to the
wisest and most gifted leaders on the planet. Any
question you had, they knew the answer; any
problem that arose, they had experience. If this were
offered to people today, they would be queueing (if
they were British) to get through the doors. Wisdom
personified is what we have through the life of Christ
and the presence of the Holy Spirit – complete with
undisturbed, endless access.

Last week, we looked at the power *of* the promise;
this week, we explore power *within* the promise.
Within Christ dwells all that we need for all that we
may encounter. For the single mum wondering how to
manage her household – He knows; for the business
woman uncertain whether or not to take this new job
– He knows; for the grandmother wondering what this
retirement season holds – He knows; for the woman
longing for children – He knows; for the wife wondering
how to carry on in this marriage – He knows. There is no
question outside His understanding and no circumstance
beyond His grace. The promises of God can shift us from
the impossible to the obtainable.

Navigating this life is not for the faint-hearted but is
for the courageous woman who refuses to back down,
sit down, give up or walk away from the mountain that
she faces. She refuses to accept the status quo or let
regret have the final word. Instead, she sets her face
like flint, takes a deep breath and believes for a new
beginning. She knows her questions will never threaten
His security, so she approaches the throne room with
expectancy. This woman is *you* – what will you ask?

**For prayer
and reflection**

**Lord, I believe You
have wise counsel
for my many
questions, and
I trust You for
direction. I place
my unknown future
safely within Your
guidance, peace
and wisdom. Amen.**

My sister's **shoes**

Isaiah 30:21;
John 16:13

'your ears will hear
a voice behind you,
saying, "This is the
way; walk in it."'
(Isa. 30:21)

When we were children, my older sister and I accidentally got ourselves locked in a closet. What started out as two giggling girls hiding from their parents, became full-blown trauma for this little girl with a big imagination. I elaborate more in my book *Face to Face** but suffice to say, our adventure culminated in me hyperventilating and vomiting all over my sister's shoes!

Darkness can be frightening – literally and metaphorically – but knowing there is one who refuses to leave us in that place makes the darkness slightly less brutal. Christ is our counsellor and our guide as we navigate the dark valleys of life. He is the good shepherd who leads His sheep; but, as Isaiah reminds us, He is also our rear guard ready to direct and correct when needed. My big sister was a calming presence who knew we would eventually be found. Like my sister, Jesus assures us that He will stay with us in that dark, confusing place as long as necessary.

Does the Christmas season create any 'dark closet' moments for you? Being single and living in a country not my own has meant numerous Christmas Days spent with other families. Experiencing various family traditions has been a blessing, but equally a reminder of what I do not have. It is easy to feel alone and isolated, so I intentionally focus on my (numerous) blessings during this season, allowing their light to shatter any impending darkness. If you find yourself feeling alone today, please look around. I believe that in place of small, vomit-covered shoes, you may see a pair of beautiful, nail-scarred shepherd's feet standing nearby.

*Face to Face, Jen Baker (Milton Keynes: Authentic Media, 2019)

For prayer and reflection

Lord, You have promised never to leave me. Thank You for standing nearby, especially in the dark places. Yours is the hand I choose to hold – today and forever. Amen.

Catherine Wilkins

Catherine talks to Inspiring Women about how following Jesus impacts every area of her life – whether she's cooking, singing, or serving the NHS on the front lines during a global pandemic…

Jesus is everything to me. He has always proved faithful, even when life has been tough or I haven't known which way to turn next. He is my motivation to be the best I can be, wherever He has placed me – whether that be in my neighbourhood, church, friendship groups or work. I firmly believe that my faith is not about Sunday and church but about all of my life.

Jesus placed a passion for nursing and midwifery in me at a young age, and I have been privileged to work in

so many different roles and hospitals within our amazing NHS. My current role within our Trust means that, at the height of the coronavirus pandemic, I was responsible for redeploying nearly 900 staff from their normal areas of work to many other areas around the hospital. This included training and moving a lot of staff to work in critical care, some of whom had never worked in that area before. My team worked tirelessly to ensure that the transition was as smooth as possible. We undertook a phenomenal workforce transformation in about three weeks! I also led on strategic workforce modelling for the region as well as our hospital. As the pandemic was unfolding so quickly, there were moments when it was all quite overwhelming. Throughout those weeks, I felt such a sense of God's peace despite the whirling world around me. The verse I have really held onto at this time is Philippians 4:13: 'I can do all things through Christ who strengthens me' (NKJV). I know He is always with me and has placed me right where I'm meant to be. I've also had opportunities to have conversations with colleagues about God and my faith, as lots of people are looking for meaning in life and seeking security in a world that is ever-changing, at times almost unrecognisable.

*'I firmly believe that my faith is not about Sunday and church but about **all** of my life.'*

I have felt the presence of God so tangibly at this time – more than I have in a really long time. I have always known God is there and trusted Him, but there have been times when He has felt more distant (or I have felt more distant from Him), and I have just had to trust in His Word and in who He is.

Worship has also been a lifeline for me. I feel alive when I sing! Singing in all forms is very good for you (scientific fact), but there is something about singing in worship that adds another dimension. I *love* to worship by singing to our amazing King. He has blessed me with a singing voice and it is my pleasure to use it to worship Him. I love being in a worship space (personal or corporate) where I can sing spontaneously whatever comes into my mind – whether that is praise or thanks or lament, singing is my way of expressing myself.

Another thing I love to do is support the youth in our church when they go to a summer festival each year. I first got involved with the young people through my love of cooking. My kitchen is my happy place, and I have extended that now to 'camping cooking' at the festivals (this would have been my fifth year). I really, *really* do not like camping, so it is a major thing that my love for cooking supersedes my loathing of camping! I love doing it because, for me, it enables our young people to be free to focus on growing in their relationships with God and having time to be together and have lots of fun. Good food (and plenty of it!) means that the basics of life are covered and they are free to do everything else. I have also been encouraged that my team are role-modelling serving, and serving with a good heart (we cooks have lots of fun too!).

Parachute of **God's grace**

Psalm 23

'I will fear no evil,
for you are with
me; your rod and
your staff, they
comfort me.' (v4)

Compassion, comfort and companionship are three 'C's promised within the poetry of Psalm 23. But packaged within this psalm is another 'C', which often goes unnoticed: choice.

Daily we can choose to receive God's compassion, comfort and companionship – or not. Notice how David said, 'I will fear no evil'; he intentionally *chose* not to fear. One of my most poignant moments of fear was standing at the edge of an open door, 15,000 feet above the ground, teetering between the safety of an aeroplane and the freedom of the free-fall. Stepping into the open air abandoned all control: my life was wholly and completely in the hands of a man I had met a few hours earlier. Trusting another person is scary, and trusting the unknown can be terrifying. But once the free-fall finished, the parachute opened and the silence overpowered all sound, the beauty of what I could see was astounding.

Skydiving can imitate 'valley' seasons in life. We are free-falling into what feels chaotic, confusing and never ending... until suddenly a change occurs and time stands still. At that moment, though possibly still in a tenuous position, we find ourselves being carried by a grace outside of ourselves. The safety harness of God's grace promises comfort in times of pain, compassion in times of confusion, and companionship in seasons of loneliness – holding us tightly until we are safely on the ground of our next season. If this season has felt like free-falling, hold on and avoid the temptation to sever the cord between you and your future promise. Given time, you *will* return to solid ground.

For prayer and reflection

If the cords of God's grace are compassion, comfort and companionship, do any need to be reattached between you and Him? Spend some time in prayer about this.

Confusion to **clarity**

**Luke 1:26–38;
Philippians
4:6–8**

'Not one promise
from God is
empty of power,
for nothing is
impossible with
God!' (Luke 1:37,
TPT)

Within moments Mary went from a confusing reality ('I am a virgin') to a clarifying purpose ('I am the Lord's servant'). We will all have seasons in life when we are called to trust a promise over confusion. Mary did this by trusting the voice of an angel, but we have a Bible filled with thousands of promises to help us navigate our seasons – each promise signposting toward a brilliant future.

These promises are like tools in a tool chest, with each one carrying power and potential to create change – but the outcome depends on the one in possession of the tool. Thankfully, we are not alone. The Holy Spirit is always standing by, ready to share counsel because haphazardly quoting scriptures can be like grabbing tools blindfolded. If we cannot see, we cannot strategise, and without strategy we are left wishing for an outcome, not expecting one.

We have the Holy Spirit to assist us on our journey, but Mary was given a companion in Elizabeth. Although Elizabeth held questions of her own, she also brought with her maturity and experience – both important tools to comfort Mary in the early days. None of us have all that we need for the journey; God has designed us to need Him *and* need one another to fulfil our purpose in life.

Like Mary, have you ever been interrupted by a gift you were not seeking? Or is your experience more like Elizabeth – divinely interrupted by a dream you had long released?

Divine interruptions will happen in this lifetime, but remember that when they do we are not alone. There will always be a promise, and a companion, ready to walk us to the other side.

**For prayer
and reflection**

Lord, You are
never confused,
so I ask now for the
peace that passes
all understanding
to guard my heart
and my mind as
I walk through
this season of
uncertainty. Amen.

Big **picture**

Lamentations 3:22; Matthew 2:1–12

'Because of the LORD'S great love we are not consumed, for his compassions never fail.' (Lam. 3:22)

For prayer and reflection

What promise has been your guiding star in life? Write it down, spending time meditating again on its truth, thanking God for His comfort in this season of life.

Tension is not always negative. A good counsellor manages the critical tension of where we are currently and where we could be eventually. In the same way, promises from God hold a tension by equally anchoring *and* freeing us. The Bible says we are meant to stand (Eph. 6:13) and having done everything stand; but it also says to walk by faith (2 Cor. 5:7). Do I stand or do I walk? Both. Consider the wise men who followed a star – they stood on their beliefs, ignoring Herod, but they also walked by their faith, worshipping Jesus.

I love the fact that stars, on a clear night, will shine regardless of where we are in this world. Living thousands of miles from my family, this knowledge is a beautiful gift to me when I feel homesick. Looking up, I smile, knowing that the stars I see in that moment, my family may be viewing several hours later. It creates connection where an ocean causes division – keeping me anchored to family and released to purpose. When I moved overseas, I needed the promises of God to hold me within the grace of God, because it's easy to question our decisions when the clouds of doubt block the light. Just as our inability to see the stars does not negate their presence, a promise slow in coming does not negate its power.

If you are standing before a door of opportunity, questioning the wisdom of walking through, ask for a promise – then stand on that promise, refusing to move, for as long as it takes. As Abraham believed against all hope that he would have many descendants (Gen. 22:17–18) and Mary witnessed a miracle against all odds, we must remain in our tension of belief, until the clouds move and our future shines bright once again.

Choose your words

. . . .

James 1:19–26

'take note of this: everyone should be quick to listen, slow to speak and slow to become angry' (v19)

I looked up the meaning of the word 'everyone' in Greek and it means… everyone! Therefore none of us are exempt from watching our words. (I know – annoying.)

James takes this challenge a step further by exhorting us not only to hear the Word, but to *obey* the Word. I believe there is a clear correlation between the two: the more we study the eternal Word (Jesus), the easier it becomes to obey the written Word (Bible).

In the mentoring sessions I have led, I've often noticed that many people focus on who they are not, instead of who they are; or what they lack, instead of what they have. I often challenge them to reframe their perspective, seeing it from the other side. For example, instead of an insecure woman trying to become confident, I encourage her to view herself as Christ sees her (healthy, confident) and then act accordingly. Because we become what we behold.

If we continually speak negatively about ourselves, choosing positively will be impossible. What would it look like for you to speak life, faith and hope over your future? Take time to imagine this picture and then seal it with prayer.

. . . .

Optional further reading

1 Peter 3:10; Colossians 4:6; Ephesians 4:29; Psalm 141:3

Mighty God

Ephesians
1:3–6,17–21; 6:10

'his incomparably great power for us who believe.' (v19)

Warrior. Valiant. Champion. These are a few alternative descriptors of the Hebrew word *Gibbor*, meaning 'mighty'. They describe a God who cannot be beaten, unafraid of battle, great in power and secure in dominion. The Hebrew word *Gibbor* describes heroes like Nimrod who was 'a mighty warrior... before the LORD' (Gen. 10:8–9) and the 'mighty warriors' of King David (2 Sam. 23:8).

When Jesus – the ultimate *Gibbor* warrior – was born as a baby, His power came not from size but from purpose. The same is true for us: being led by purpose, we will find our worth in how we are viewed by heaven, not how we are viewed on earth. Our worth is not based on our bank account, marital status or popularity on social media. Instead, our sense of worth comes from being placed 'in Christ'. Therefore, when the Father looks at us, He sees the Son; equally, when the enemy attacks us, he faces the Son. It is an amazing thought: at this moment, you rest in the centre of the safest, and yet most power-filled, place you could ever hope to be: in Christ.

This week we will explore the power *behind* the promise – a power not dependent on physical might, perfect conditions or a weak opponent; a power that never backs down but remains ever-present and always working. When we stand on God's many promises, we are holding fast to a truth backed by heaven. Remember David running towards Goliath without fear or hesitation (1 Sam. 17:48)? David knew the power backing his promise guaranteed his victory, so he was quick to trust and take action. Knowing that Jesus, the mighty *Gibbor* warrior, stands behind you, will you run with the same confidence toward your Goliath?

For prayer and reflection

Lord, You are more powerful than any fear, disease, sin or battle that I face today. Please help me trust the mighty power behind that promise until I see victory. Amen.

Blessed is the believer

Jesus is mighty in battle *and* mighty in blessing, but we can miss the blessing if distracted by the battle.

I recently fought a persistent virus (separate to the pandemic), and within days I could no longer remember what healthy felt like. It showed me that if my expectations are not met, my focus can easily be distorted. For example, if I need perfect conditions to sing in church, then my praise will be rare indeed; if I want all my needs met before I help another, then I do not understand the heart of giving; if the other person must apologise first, then I miss the beautiful gift of forgiveness.

Often, in times of great challenge, sacrifice is required but, equally, blessing is experienced. My favourite definition of the word blessing is 'empowered to prosper'. I love the idea of heaven coming behind a promise, unlocking blessing and releasing a prosperity that extends beyond us into the lives of others. Isn't that why we are blessed – to be a blessing? The truth is that promise and blessing will always be present; by choosing them we are not denying the pain, we are amplifying the promise.

If our lives only contained what we thanked God for this morning, how much would we have? Would we still have our health? Home? Family? Relationships? It is a sobering thought and a good reminder that, in spite of challenges, we are a blessed people. One day there will be no more tears or sorrow but pure, unadulterated joy, love and peace will be our *forever* home. If we are distracted by the battle and struggling to praise, let's begin with the end in mind – thank Him for heaven so you can trust Him on earth.

**Matthew 5:1–12;
Luke 1:45**

'Blessed is she who has believed that the Lord would fulfill his promises to her!' (Luke 1:45)

For prayer and reflection

Thank God for your blessings and then pray for someone who is struggling to find joy in this season. Perhaps send them a note letting them know you are thinking of them.

The **wave**

Jeremiah 29:11;
John 6:38

'For I know the plans I have for you' (Jer. 29:11)

P urpose is a journey, not a destination. I imagine our life purpose forming like a tidal wave: it begins without shape... gains momentum as time passes... takes on a life of its own... and eventually overtakes those in its path and beyond. The birth of Christ was similar: agreeing in heaven to become a sacrifice, arriving as a baby, growing in wisdom, leaving a meteoric imprint that continues to impact generations.

Irrespective of how large you feel your 'wave' might be, it is impossible to pursue the will of God without leaving a legacy because God never wastes a seeking heart. Yes, one fingerprint may be larger than another but *together* we leave a mark that shapes eternity. The fingerprint of a man named Edward Kimball may not seem impressive, but Edward led D.L. Moody (a man who shared the gospel with over 100 million people in the nineteenth century) to Christ. D.L. Moody highly influenced J. Wilbur Chapman, who, in turn, strongly influenced a man named Billy Sunday. Billy began Christian businessmen meetings, and at one of these Mordecai Ham was invited to speak. At another of Mordecai's meetings, another man, Billy Graham, went forward to make a deeper commitment to Christ – and the rest, as they say, is history.

Who can say which fingerprint had the deepest impact? That is like judging which drop of water produced the greatest impact from the tidal wave – it was the combined unity, not the individual, that made the difference. In His teaching, Jesus regularly pointed His listeners to the one who sent Him – His Father. Similarly, our purpose is not meant to draw attention to ourselves, but together, with God's help, we will leave an unforgettable imprint.

For prayer and reflection

Lord, forgive me for the times when I have compared my life with others'. Help me see purpose underpinning my life today – in the prayers that I pray and the deeds that I do. Amen.

Be **love**

**1 Corinthians
13:4–7;
1 John 4:7–12**

'God is love.'
(1 John 4:8)

From the moment of birth to the point of death, Jesus looked up and searched His mother's face, finding love. Imagine the tears of joy Mary wept at His birth, unable to take her eyes off His tiny, cloudy, brown, newborn eyes; perhaps feeling as if she was in a surreal dream from which she would soon awake. Fast forward 33 years to a stormy day, standing on a hill, *her* eyes now clouded by anguish, scarcely able to see her baby – her Saviour – through tears of sorrow, witnessing a nightmare she knew was real. Even so, Mary saw God's love with a clarity future generations would struggle to understand.

Love clarifies; it helps us to focus on what is most important. The recent tragic and unexpected death of someone I knew underscored to me the reality that Earth is not our home. Each one of us has been created for a purpose, which continues after we have stopped breathing. By keeping this truth in mind, petty squabbles and errant judgments can more easily be overshadowed by love.

The #BeKind campaign was born out of a tragic, untimely death, and while I fully embrace its truth, I think we can take it further. What would it look like to 'be love' to someone today? Think about what it might look like for our acts of kindness to be rooted in a deep and sacrificial love. Kindness may not always require inconvenience, but love requires us to leave our world and step into the world of another.

This type of mighty, *Gibbor* love originated from Jesus. His love will never leave or forsake us and will stay with us from birth into eternity. Mary chose this love. Will we?

**For prayer
and reflection**

Lord, in the midst of my busyness, stress and frustration, I choose to love You. Help me see what is most important, trusting You today with my anxious questions. Amen.

No more shame

**2 Corinthians
12:1–10;
Ephesians 2:8–9**

'My grace is
sufficient for you'
(2 Cor. 12:9)

Years ago, a friend shared with me about a pastoral visit that went terribly wrong. She was given a cup of tea that tasted so awful my friend quickly poured the tea into a plant pot when the host stepped out of the room. She was trying to avoid embarrassing the host, so this seemed an appropriate solution. But, in her haste, my friend overlooked the obvious: it was a fake plant. Unable to own up to her actions, she made a quick exit and never spoke of the incident to the plant owner!

This is a minor, yet humorous, example of a major issue – the power of shame to keep us in a prison where we do not belong. Owning up to her actions would have been the right thing to do. However, there are times in life when, for whatever reason, we feel unable to face the unfaceable. In those times, I am most in awe of the grace of God. His mighty grace was made available on the cross through Jesus' blood, empowering our promise of salvation, redemption and eternal life. We tend to think of grace mostly on two occasions – when we have sinned, and Easter Sunday – but grace is available each and every day, waiting to cleanse and ready to empower.

**For prayer
and reflection**

**Are you currently
struggling to
forgive someone,
or perhaps accept
forgiveness
yourself? Ask God
to help you to offer
or receive grace as
you need to today.**

God's grace brings freedom, and our grace (through faith extending favour and kindness) blesses others. As Christmas Day approaches, set time aside to meditate on this beautiful gift of grace – undeserved, yet freely given. As you do, become aware of your breathing while you imagine yourself breathing in His grace and breathing out your shame.

Finally, consider if there is anyone you need to extend grace towards today... perhaps over a cup of tea?

Weekend

Choose your actions

Matthew 1:18–25

We can easily forget that Joseph was human like us, with emotions, fears, doubts and dreams. Imagine how he felt when Mary approached him with the news that she was pregnant. Joseph, of course, didn't have our advantage of knowing the story's ending through reading the Gospels – all of these events were in 'real time' for him. Perhaps he had feelings of anger, fear and confusion, but the choices Joseph made shaped eternity. He dismissed the obvious choice and chose the obedient one.

The angel told Joseph not to fear, and the word 'fear' in Greek means to withdraw, and carried with it a sense of wanting to flee. Have you ever wanted to flee a situation but instead you chose to stay and face the consequences? Joseph defied convention and stood by the woman he loved, accepting a son not conceived by him. He also honoured Mary by not consummating their marriage until after the birth – that is a man of integrity.

Our actions are *always* our choice. Therefore, choose carefully who you will serve, how you will love and the legacy you will leave because, like Joseph, today's choice becomes tomorrow's imprint.

Optional further reading
Joshua 24:15

Everlasting **Father**

**Jeremiah 31:1–6;
Revelation
21:1–6**

'I am the Alpha
and the Omega,
the Beginning
and the End.'
(Rev. 21:6)

**For prayer
and reflection**

**Notice the
moments of God's
intervention in
today's Bible
reading and
remember the
moments God
intervened in your
life this past year.
Thank Him for
those times.**

I f you want to put your brain in a twist, meditate on eternity. The thought of something never ending is nearly impossible for our finite minds to comprehend. And if you are anything like me, as much as I want to see Jesus (and I do), I am slightly anxious at the thought of *forever*. I suppose it feels a bit like a Netflix show with an unlimited amount of seasons – surely the plot must achieve a natural conclusion eventually!

During Christmas week, we will focus on the eternal promises that are ours through Christ's birth (and death), truths that are as real today as they will be a thousand years from now. No gift this Christmas, as costly as it may be, can match that durability.

Today, connect with heaven by putting down the gift wrap and stepping away from the mince pies. Close your eyes to distraction and demand, bringing perspective to a season easily hijacked by the urgent. If this time of year holds painful memories, bring those to God, resting in His grace and receiving His love. There is no need to perform in His presence. He welcomes you as you are.

Enjoy the moment, because moments are important, each one linking with another, creating an eternal mosaic. Celebrating special moments on earth is practice for life everlasting. Whether at church, home, work or the local shop, we have opportunities each day to create memorable moments. This week, in the midst of the urgent, be a blessing, not a burden; speak words of life, not of death; write scripts that last longer than a good TV series – ones that may take an eternity to finish.

Never **alone**

**Joshua 1:8–9;
Hebrews 13:5–6**

'I will never leave
you nor forsake
you.' (Josh. 1:5)

Have you ever been left behind? I remember, as a kid, running after my older sister and the neighbours' kids – I was left lagging behind, yelling for them to wait, watching them speed ahead laughing and having fun without me. I can still recall the sense of rejection and hurt. Nobody likes being left behind, or left out, and intentionally rejecting another person is cruel at any age.

One of the most beautiful promises in the Bible is the one that says we will never – ever – be fully alone. God is *always* with us, for us and never against us. In Joshua's greatest moment of testing, God promised Joshua that He was there for him, and in the New Testament, Jesus assured His disciples that He was never out of reach but with them always, until the end of the age. As many women have discovered, being alone is not simply the absence of others. We can feel alone, even when surrounded by children, husband, work colleagues or a community. In short, a sense of emptiness is no respecter of persons. Desolation must be confronted with truth and action if we want to see lasting change.

As we sing about joy coming to the world, keep an eye out for those who are alone and not experiencing joy in this season. Don't hesitate to remind them of their value and, if you can, invite them into your world for a cup of tea or Christmas treat. If you are the one feeling alone, as difficult as it is, please reach out to someone – do not remain silent. This way, as we all run our race together with Christ, we will cross the final finish line hand in hand – not one of us lagging behind.

**For prayer
and reflection**

**Lord, I ask You to
bring to mind or
open my eyes to
those who need
to know Your
love this season.
Please inspire me
with creativity in
expressing that
love to them.
Amen.**

No more **time**

'Whoever comes to me will never go hungry, and whoever believes in me will never be thirsty.' (v35)

It seems everything today has an expiration date: a pen runs out of ink, our car insurance needs renewing, the goldfish gets tired of swimming. We live in a world limited by time. Even Mary and Joseph were under a deadline to register for the census, let alone find shelter for the approaching birth of their son. With every closed door, time seemed to mock their desperation. Perhaps you can relate?

Do you feel time has run out in a relationship you once enjoyed, a dream that you have held or even in life itself? We know that as we age, time appears to accelerate but the truth is: time has not changed, we have. There have always been, and will always be, 24 hours in a day. I decide how to use that time: I can wallow over what is no longer mine or I can be in faith for what I will soon possess. Beating ourselves up or blaming God will never redeem time; conversely, it steals the time that still remains.

Despite the closed doors, Mary and Joseph never let rejection have the final word. They persevered until they found an open door and a gracious welcome. As you think about the days leading up to Christ's birth, ponder your own circumstances. Are there closed doors, which have kept you circling rejection, condemnation or frustration for too long? As with Jesus' parents, see each closed door bringing you closer to the perfectly planned setting for your next season. The setting where you are accepted, provided for and enabled to begin again.

The end of Mary's childhood brought forth her child's beginning – setting a plan in motion that expired death once and for all. When have you experienced new birth from a finished season?

For prayer and reflection

Lord, I bring to You my sorrow over relationships or dreams that expired before I felt ready. Thank You for hearing my cries and receiving my hurt. Amen.

Next Issue

January

PRESENCE

CHRIS LEONARD

February

RESTORING OUR CUTTING EDGE

ANNE LE TISSIER

Also available as eBook/eSubscription

In **January**, Chris Leonard considers some of the ways God's presence was made known throughout the Bible, and how we can experience it in our own lives, while also being present to Him and to others in the year ahead.

In **February**, Anne Le Tissier unpacks the unusual story of the floating axehead in 2 Kings 6, likening it to our spiritual 'cutting edge', and how God can restore us when we feel like we've lost our sense of purpose, direction and effectiveness.

Obtain your copy from CWR, Christian bookshops or your National Distributor. Please note: from the next issue, the price of your copy will be £3.49. For updated subscription prices, please see the order form at the back of these notes.

New **life**

'I came that they may have… life, and have it in abundance (to the full, till it overflows).' (John 10:10, AMPC)

For prayer and reflection

Ask God to reveal three people who you can intentionally encourage today through written or spoken words. If this is difficult, instead, spend time praying for them.

T
he generosity of God will never lessen, lighten or be limited; it is free-flowing now and throughout eternity.

God has never thought to Himself: *I cannot afford that. That is a bit too much to spend on her. She is not worth my best.* On the contrary, He is an abundant God always seeking opportunities to furnish His daughters with blessings. He cannot help but overflow with love because that is the nature of love.

While clear blessings from heaven are fun to receive, God also packages gifts in less obvious wrapping; for example, in the homeless man asking for help, the child acting up while trying to find their way or the relative hurting us out of their own hurt. These 'gifts' are hidden opportunities for us to be His hands and feet as we overflow with the kindness, wisdom and forgiveness we have so abundantly received. The Amplified translation of John 10:10 paints this picture beautifully, showing an overflowing life so full that it cannot be contained within the boundaries of our current desires. Are you living an overflowing life?

Whether you are spending Christmas with family, friends or it's you and Jesus this year, be aware of the eternal gifts that you have inherited. Look for others in need of refreshment, being generous in what you give, not solely focused on what you will receive. Let's not let the obvious gifts distract us from the greater ones. Extravagance is found in the nature of God, so live extravagantly, remembering that God's nature also shows us that the most meaningful packages are made of memories, not purchased with money.

The **Word**

John 1:1–5,14;
Hebrews 1:1–3

'In the beginning
was the Word'
(John 1:1)

Today we celebrate the birth of a new sound – the sound of everlasting freedom. From His inaugural infant cry to the anguished final declaration, Jesus Christ answered the wearied groans of creation by stepping into our world as the living Word. He was the Word before the incarnation and He is the Word now seated at the right hand of God – He was, He is and He will forever be our eternal Word.

A.W. Tozer has reminded us that God is not a silent God but one who desires to speak to any who desire to listen. He is not solely meant to be studied but to be explored and known through relationship and the written Word of God. Phillips Brooks says, 'The Bible is like a *telescope*. If a man looks *through* his telescope, then he sees the *worlds beyond*; but if he only looks *at* his telescope, then he does not see anything but that. The Bible is to be *looked through*, to see that which is beyond; but most people only look at it; and so they see only the dead letter.'* What has the Word illuminated to you this month? This season?

As we celebrate the eternal Word today, listen to the lyrics heaven sings over you: holy, blessed, favoured, loved, redeemed, wanted, welcomed, healed, adopted and free. Let's remember that people can hold an opinion of our worth, but only the Saviour *defines* our worth – on that subject, He is never silent.

So, however you are celebrating the birth of our amazing Saviour today, let this special day resound with the sounds of heaven: love, freedom, peace and joy. Happy Christmas!

*HELPS Word, available at thediscoverybible.com

**For prayer
and reflection**

Lord, words
cannot express my
gratitude for Your
decision to come
as a helpless baby.
I celebrate You
today as the living,
true, eternal and
beautiful Word.
Amen.

Choose your beliefs

Acts 4:11–13,23–31

'enable your servants to speak your word with great boldness.'
(Acts 4:29)

Years ago, I sat at a table with 18 other pastors as we discussed possible solutions for an issue at our church. My heart was beating rapidly as I had what I believed was the perfect solution, but I was too afraid to speak, so I remained silent. Numerous suggestions were tossed around with no apparent solution, until another pastor voiced *my* plan. Hearing her suggestion, the leader commended her for her brilliance, and everyone agreed that this was an ideal way forward. I wanted to scream, 'I thought of it first!', but of course I couldn't say anything, because I hadn't said anything.

I quickly learned that when I abdicate my responsibility to speak, God will find somebody else to do the job. I never wanted that to happen again and, although not perfect, I seek to use my voice for His glory whenever the opportunity arises, even if it's done with fear and trembling.

Despite all the goodness and kindness you see, the world also has an abundance of prejudice and judgment, but it is time – as in the days of the Early Church – for the Bride of Christ to speak the words of heaven without shame and with authority. What will you say?

....

Optional further reading
Hebrews 11

Prince of **Peace**

P eace was never meant to be circumstance dependent; it is a lifestyle. We know that worldly peace is often based on good news, perfect conditions, a favourable diagnosis or an abundance of possessions. But peace in the kingdom supersedes the trappings of circumstance, placing us in the heart of tranquillity regardless of storm, trial or danger.

While peace is a product of our relationship with our Father, the level of peace we have will be influenced by the amount of control we release to Him, because control and faith cannot cohabit. When Jesus said in John 14:27, 'Do not let your hearts be troubled', He knew that would be easier if they meditated on, and believed, the *first* part of that scripture: 'Peace I leave with you; my peace I give you.'

Did you catch that? We can stop anxiety in its tracks by receiving what Jesus is offering: *His own peace.* But it remains our responsibility to trust that gift more than our fear. The more we practise this discipline, the easier it becomes to stop trouble and anxiety from invading our hearts.

As we approach another new year, let's review this past one by asking ourselves these questions: where did the Lord challenge my comfort zone? Did I allow peace a voice in that season? Have I struggled to obey God in any area?

We can learn an important lesson about peace and obedience from Mary and Joseph, who stared into the eyes of their newborn – loving Him as a child, yet knowing He was a King. The responsibility must have felt overwhelming but their sacrificial obedience paved the way for us to hold today what they beheld that day – perfect peace.

2 Thessalonians 3:16; Colossians 3:12–17

'may the Lord of peace himself give you peace at all times and in every way.' (2 Thess. 3:16)

For prayer and reflection

Lord, I choose to let Your peace speak louder than my fear, declaring 'Peace be still' over my life, heart, family, health and finances. Thank You for Your perfect peace. Amen.

A **heart** speaks

Galatians
5:13–25; 6:7–8

'Since we live by
the Spirit, let us
keep in step with
the Spirit.' (v25)

I f you could relive your conversations from yesterday, what words would you change? This month we have seen the promised child and His promises through the lens of counsel, might, eternity and peace. Jesus not only demonstrated peace in the storm, He showed us peace as the norm. It was His mode of operation on a daily basis: comforting a grieving mother; wiping shame off the face of a Samaritan woman; calling the bleeding woman 'daughter'; and reinstating a disciple who had gone rogue. Words of love, affirmation, acceptance and life flowed from His lips every day.

It is a biblical truth that out of the overflow of the heart the mouth speaks, so the obvious question would be: have you listened to your heart lately? How do you speak to your loved ones when you are tired, to your employees when you are frustrated or to your friends when they let you down? We are tempted to focus on the other person but the Bible highlights our own hearts; it never excuses wrong words because of another person's bad behaviour.

Jesus has given us the necessary tools to be a peace-giver where there is hate, violence, judgment and prejudice; but we cannot reap what we have not planted. Change requires a voice: Martin Luther King Jr influenced a movement; Aimee Semple McPherson influenced a denomination; Anne Frank influenced humanity; Sojourner Truth influenced prejudice; Deborah influenced an army; a Samaritan woman influenced a city. They each made a choice for change.

Yesterday is gone but today carries with it fresh opportunity. Will you speak today what you wished you had said yesterday?

**For prayer
and reflection**

**Think about your
conversations
recently – would
you adjust any,
if you could? Ask
for forgiveness,
if necessary,
declaring that
today you are led
by peace, not strife.**

What you **carry**

'Young man, I say
to you, get up!'
(Luke 7:14)

The day she meant to bury her past was the day He birthed her future, because a negative atmosphere never threatens a peace carrier.

This widow had lost everything – family, finances, security – but the Prince of Peace stepped into her world of turmoil, bringing restoration with only one touch. In that culture, having contact with a coffin would have been abhorrent for a rabbi, yet the peace that Jesus carried overturned the death that they were holding.

Are there 'dead' situations around you that need a touch of peace – in our communities, on social media, with the destitute? Every day we have opportunities to boycott words or actions that speak of death. Stepping away from the familiar takes courage, while approaching what has died takes faith – and peace leads us in both. Remember, the widow did not come alongside Jesus; He reached out to her. Though Christ's peace was not explicitly mentioned, it was seen through His actions. Jesus was not worried, doubtful, anxious or agitated. He simply changed the atmosphere by generously giving the healing He carried.

Paul and Silas were worshipping while the other prisoners were listening. Jesus not only freed Paul and Silas, but He also restored the jailer's entire family to wholeness. It makes me wonder what I carry into a crisis - actions that bring life or death? Do you know someone carrying a burden far too heavy, with a peace long gone, who could use your touch of faith today?

Like Jesus, the peace we carry is powerful, reaching beyond us and leaving an impact wherever we go. But we must decide to step out, approach and touch what others may deem untouchable.

**For prayer
and reflection**

Lord, please show me who needs to receive this peace that I carry. Thank You for giving me courage to touch 'dead' situations, seeing them rise to life again. Amen.

Lifestyle of peace

'Let us therefore make every effort to do what leads to peace'
(Rom. 14:19)

Maintaining peace happens by choice, not by chance. Recently I read a social media post, which included a cute, seemingly benign quote that endorsed people who woke up feeling sad to stay in bed, not wash until they felt better and to alter their day to fit their mood. I don't think that is necessarily the best way to deal with sorrow. That type of thinking can indulge self-pity and doesn't always reflect true self-care.

We are encouraged at this time of year to review our past and contemplate our future. This can be a healthy exercise but it can go terribly wrong if we, like the social media post suggested, allow our emotions to dictate our decisions. In spite of popular opinion, our emotions are not in charge – we are.

Our readings today focus on a lifestyle of peace, which we will only cultivate when we choose to live out what the Spirit of God has already put in, as seen in the life of Jesus. The enemy could not tempt Him and the Pharisees could not trap Him, He was sought after by the hungry and rebuked by the proud – yet the Prince of Peace remains the same yesterday, today and forever. That same Spirit dwells within us but we have to choose to trust its leading.

For prayer and reflection

Reviewing the promises we have studied this month, prayerfully choose one or two to carry into 2021. Write them down, intentionally keeping them before you.

This month, we have seen God become child, who became man, who became the Lamb, who became the King, empowering us to share His promises, not only at Christmas but every day. As this year takes its final bow, we close the door on 2020; but before we do, remember who eagerly waits in the wings of 2021, ready to walk centre stage of our next season: Wonderful Counsellor, Mighty God, Everlasting Father, Prince of Peace... the Promised One.

Order form

5 Easy Ways To Order

1. Phone in your credit card order: **01252 784700** (Mon–Fri, 9.30am – 4.30pm)
2. Visit our online store at **cwr.org.uk/store**
3. Send this form together with your payment to: **CWR, Waverley Abbey House, Waverley Lane, Farnham, Surrey GU9 8EP**
4. Visit a Christian bookshop
5. For Australia and New Zealand visit KI Gifts **cwr4u.net.au**

For a list of our National Distributors, who supply countries outside the UK, visit cwr.org.uk/distributors

Your Details (required for orders and donations)

Full Name:	CWR ID No. (if known):
Home Address:	
	Postcode:
Telephone No. (for queries):	Email:

Publications

TITLE	QTY	PRICE	TOTAL
		Total Publications	

UK P&P: up to £24.99 = **2.99**; £25.00 and over = **FREE**

Elsewhere P&P: up to £10 = **£4.95**; £10.01 – £50 = **£6.95**; £50.01 – £99.99 = **£10**; £100 and over = **£30**

Total Publications and P&P (please allow 14 days for delivery)	**A**	

Subscriptions* (non direct debit)

	QTY	PRICE (including P&P)			TOTAL
		UK	Europe	Elsewhere	
Every Day with Jesus (1yr, 6 issues)		£17.95	£22.50	Please contact nearest National Distributor or CWR direct	
Large Print *Every Day with Jesus* (1yr, 6 issues)		£17.95	£22.50		
Inspiring Women Every Day (1yr, 6 issues)		£17.95	£22.50		
Life Every Day (Jeff Lucas) (1yr, 6 issues)		£17.95	£22.50		
YP's: 11–14s (1yr, 6 issues)		£17.95	£22.50		
Topz: 7–11s (1yr, 6 issues)		£17.95	£22.50		
Total Subscriptions (subscription prices already include postage and packing)				**B**	

*Only use this section for subscriptions paid for by credit/debit card or cheque. For Direct Debit subscriptions see overleaf.

All CWR adult Bible reading notes are also available in **eBook** and **email subscription** format. Visit **cwr.org.uk** for further information.

Please circle which issue you would like your subscription to commence from:

JAN/FEB MAR/APR MAY/JUN JUL/AUG SEP/OCT NOV/DEC

💬 *How would you like to hear from us?*

Continued overleaf >>

We would love to keep you up to date on all aspects of the CWR ministry, including; new publications, courses and events as well as how you can support us.

If you **DO** want to hear from us on **email**, please tick here [ ]

If you **DO NOT** want us to contact you by **post**, please tick here [ ]

You can update your preferences at any time by contacting our customer services team on 01252 784 700. You can view our privacy policy online at cwr.org.uk

Payment Details

☐ I enclose a cheque made payable to CWR for the amount of: £ _____

☐ Please charge my credit/debit card.

Cardholder's Name (in BLOCK CAPITALS) _____

Card No. ☐☐☐☐ ☐☐☐☐ ☐☐☐☐ ☐☐☐☐

Expires End ☐☐ ☐☐

Security Code ☐☐☐

Gift to CWR ☐ Please send me an acknowledgement of my gift   C ☐

Gift Aid (your home address required, see overleaf)

giftaid it I am a UK taxpayer and want CWR to reclaim the tax on all my donations for the four years prior to this year **and on** all donations I make from the date of this Gift Aid declaration until further notice.*

Taxpayer's Full Name (in BLOCK CAPITALS) _____

Signature _____ **Date** _____

*I am a UK taxpayer and understand that if I pay less Income Tax and/or Capital Gains Tax than the amount of Gift Aid claimed on all my donations in that tax year it is my responsibility to pay any difference.

GRAND TOTAL (Total of A, B & C) ☐

Subscriptions by Direct Debit (UK bank account holders only)

One-year subscriptions (6 issues a year) cost £17.95 and include UK delivery. Please tick relevant boxes and fill in the form below.

		Issue to commence from		
☐ *Every Day with Jesus*	☐ *Life Every Day* (Jeff Lucas)	☐ Jan/Feb	☐ May/Jun	☐ Sep/Oct
☐ Large Print *Every Day with Jesus*	☐ *YP's*: 11–14s	☐ Mar/Apr	☐ Jul/Aug	☐ Nov/Dec
☐ *Inspiring Women Every Day*	☐ *Topz*: 7–11s			

CWR Instruction to your Bank or Building Society to pay by Direct Debit

DIRECT Debit

Please fill in the form and send to: CWR, Waverley Abbey House, Waverley Lane, Farnham, Surrey GU9 8EP

Name and full postal address of your Bank or Building Society

To: The Manager _____ Bank/Building Society

Address _____

_____

_____

Postcode _____

Name(s) of Account Holder(s)

_____

Branch Sort Code

☐☐ ☐☐ ☐☐

Bank/Building Society Account Number

☐☐☐☐☐☐☐☐

Originator's Identification Number

4	2	0	4	8	7

Reference

☐☐☐☐☐☐☐☐☐☐☐☐☐☐☐☐☐☐

Instruction to your Bank or Building Society

Please pay CWR Direct Debits from the account detailed in this Instruc subject to the safeguards assured by the Direct Debit Guarantee.
I understand that this Instruction may remain with CWR and, if so, deta will be passed electronically to my Bank/Building Society.

Signature(s)

_____

Date

_____

Banks and Building Societies may not accept Direct Debit Instructions for some types of account